Stories from the Quran
Book 5

Mary *(Maryam)* and the Angel
&
Baby Jesus *(Isa)* Speaks

written by **Dalia Salaam** *edited by* **Noura Durkee**

illustrated by
Fatima Masood

HOOD HOOD BOOKS

Mary and the Angel

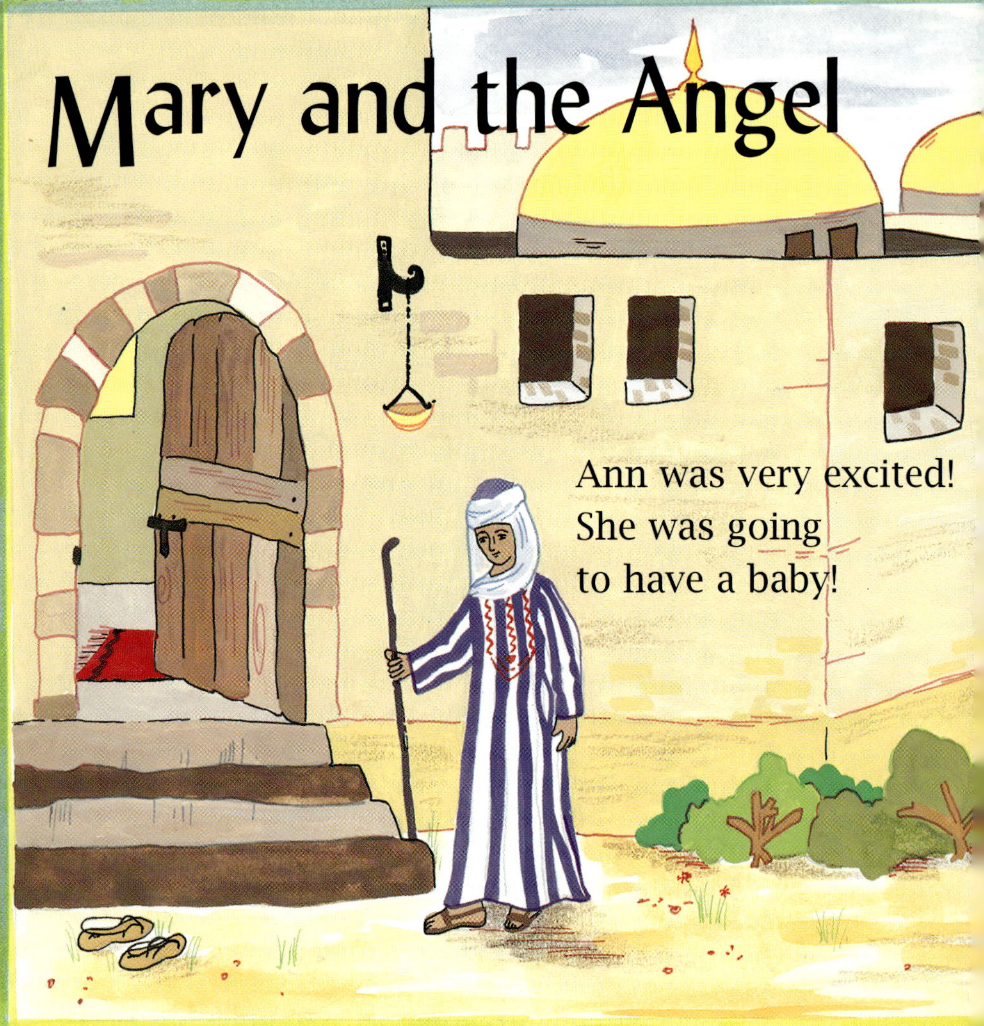

Ann was very excited!
She was going
to have a baby!

She made a promise to give
the baby to God.
This meant the child would
grow up in the temple.
That was where the people
studied and prayed.

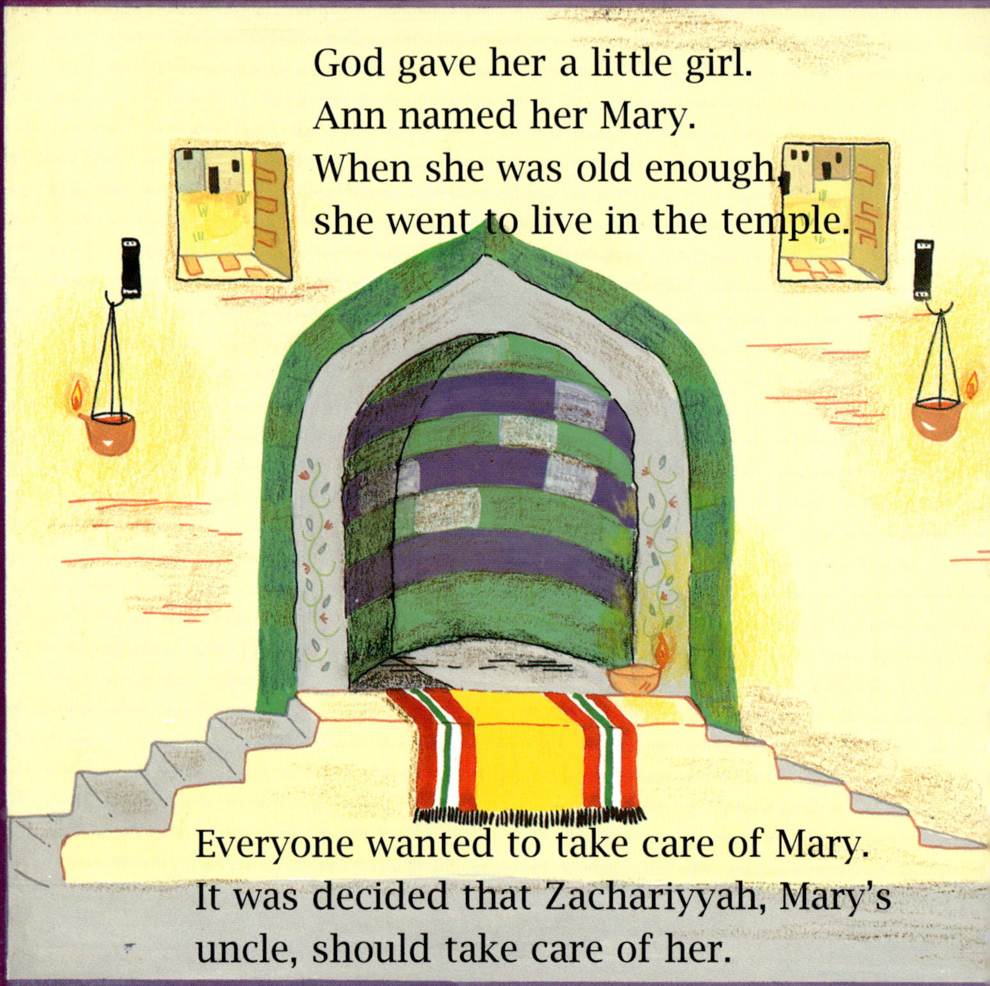

God gave her a little girl.
Ann named her Mary.
When she was old enough,
she went to live in the temple.

Everyone wanted to take care of Mary.
It was decided that Zachariyyah, Mary's
uncle, should take care of her.

Zachariyyah was a very holy man.
As it was God's wish,
he made a special place in the temple
for Mary to pray.

One night while she was praying,
Mary saw a flash of light.
Suddenly, an Angel
named Gabriel appeared.

Mary was very scared.

The Angel said,
"Mary, do not be afraid.
I have come as a
Messenger from God
to tell you that you are
going to have a special son."

Mary was amazed that God had
chosen her to have this baby.
She was very happy.

She was also very worried.
What would people say
when she had a baby
who had no father?

Mary decided to leave the temple,
and go to a quiet place to have her baby.

This special baby would
become a great Prophet.

Baby Jesus
Speaks

Mary sat under a palm tree to
have her baby.
She was all alone.
She was hungry and scared.
Then she heard a voice say,

"Mary, do not be sad.
God is taking care of you.
Shake this tree
and dates will fall for you to eat.
There is a nice stream at your feet.
Drink!"

Mary did as the
voice said.

Mary had a beautiful baby boy,
just as the Angel Gabriel had told her.

She named him Jesus.
This was the name God wanted.

Mary decided to return home.
She wondered what to tell
her family and friends.

When Mary reached her home
with Baby Jesus,
people shouted at her, saying,
"You are a bad woman!"

Mary just put her
finger to her lips,
then pointed to her baby.

They laughed and said,
"How can we talk with a baby?!"

Just then, Baby Jesus began to speak!
He said, “I am the Servant of God.
God has blessed me and made me a Prophet.
He has made me kind to my mother.”

The people were very surprised. "Wow! This is a real miracle!" they said. "This baby is not like other babies!"

The people knew then
that Baby Jesus
was sent from God.

They did not ask Mary any
more questions.
They were kind to her.
Mary was very happy
to be back home.

Hood Hood Books
46 Clabon Mews
London SW1X 0EH

Tel 44 (0) 20 7584 7878
Fax: 44 (0) 20 7225 0386·
E-mail: info@hoodhood.com
Web Site: www.hoodhood.com

British Library Cataloguing-in-Publication Data
A catalogue record for this book is available from the British Library

ISBN 1 900251 60 4

Origination by *Fine Line Graphics Ltd.* - London
Printed by *Khai Wah-Ferco Pte. Ltd.* - Singapore

PUBLISHER'S NOTE

According to the *hadith* (saying) of the Prophet Muhammad, peace be upon him, it is traditional practice not to depict God's Angels, Messengers and Prophets in any form of visual representation. There are no such depictions in this book.